W9-CRF-955

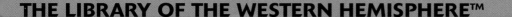

Exploring MEXICO

with the FIVE Themes of Geography

by Nancy Golden

The Rosen Publishing Group
PowerKids Press™
New York

Published in 2005 by The Rosen Publishing Group, Inc.
29 East 21st Street, New York, NY 10010

Copyright © 2005 by The Rosen Publishing Group, Inc.

All rights reserved. No part of this book may be reproduced in any form without permission in writing from the publisher, except by a reviewer.

First Edition

Editor: Geeta Sobha
Book Design: Michelle Innes

Photo Credits: Cover, p. 1 © Keith Wood/Getty Images; pp. 9, 12 © Royalty-Free/Corbis; p. 9 (Cabo San Lucas) © Mike Brinson/Getty Images; p. 9 (Agua Azul) © Nik Wheeler/Corbis; p. 10 © Mike Kelly/Getty Images; p. 10 (butterflies) © George Lepp/Getty Images; p. 10 (gila monster) © Tim Flach/Getty Images; p. 12 (mariachi) © David Seawell/Corbis; p. 15 © Lonnie Duka/Getty Images; p. 15 (Cancun) © Bob Krist/Corbis; p. 16 © Lynsey Addario/Corbis; p. 16 (Mexico City) © Stephanie Maze/Corbis; p. 19 © Dave G. Houser/Corbis; p. 19 (rural road) © Roger Ressmeyer/Corbis; p. 21 © Corbis

Library of Congress Cataloging-in-Publication Data

Golden, Nancy.
    Exploring Mexico with the five themes of geography / by Nancy Golden.— 1st ed.
    p. cm. — (The library of the Western Hemisphere)
    Includes index.
    ISBN 1-4042-2668-0 (lib. bdg.) — ISBN 0-8239-4628-2 (pbk.)
    1. Mexico—Geography—Juvenile literature. I. Title. II. Series.

F1210.9.G65 2005
917.2—dc22

                                                      2004004912

Manufactured in the United States of America

Contents

The FIVE Themes of Geography

To study the geography of Earth, we look at its people, climate, resources, and physical features. The five themes of geography—location, place, human-environment interaction, movement, and regions—are used to study particular countries or areas. These themes are used to help us understand and organize information about places around the world. Let's see how the five themes of geography can help us learn about Mexico.

1 Location

Where is Mexico?

Mexico can be found by using its absolute, or exact, location. Absolute location tells exactly where a place is in the world. The imaginary lines of longitude and latitude are used to give a place its absolute location.

Relative, or general, location is also used to define where a place is. Relative location tells where a place is in relation to other places around it. The cardinal points of east, west, north, and south are also used to show relative location.

2 Place

What is Mexico like?

To really know Mexico, we have to look at its physical and human features. Physical features are things, such as bodies of water, landforms, climate, and animal and plant life, that occur in nature. Human features are things, such as cities, buildings, government, and traditions, that have been created by people.

3 Human-Environment Interaction

How do the people and the environment of Mexico affect each other?

Human-environment interaction deals with how the land has shaped the way people live in Mexico. Also, this theme explains how the people of Mexico have changed their environment or adapted to it.

4 Movement

How do people, goods, and ideas get from place to place in Mexico?

This theme explains how products, people, and ideas move from place to place in Mexico. It can also show how they move from Mexico to other places around the world.

5 Regions

What does Mexico have in common with other places around the world? What features do places within Mexico share to make them part of a region?

Places are grouped into regions by physical and cultural features that they share. This theme studies the features that Mexico shares with other areas, making it part of a certain region. Also, it looks at political and physical regions within Mexico.

The absolute location of Mexico is 23° north and 102° west.

Mexico is bordered on the north by the United States. On the southeast, it is bordered by Guatemala and Belize. The Pacific Ocean lies to the west and south of the country. On the east is the Gulf of Mexico.

Where in the World?

Absolute location is the point where the lines of longitude and latitude meet.

Longitude tells a place's position in degrees east or west of the prime meridian, a line that runs through Greenwich, London.

Latitude tells a place's position in degrees north or south of the equator, the imaginary line that goes around the middle of the earth.

102°west

23°north

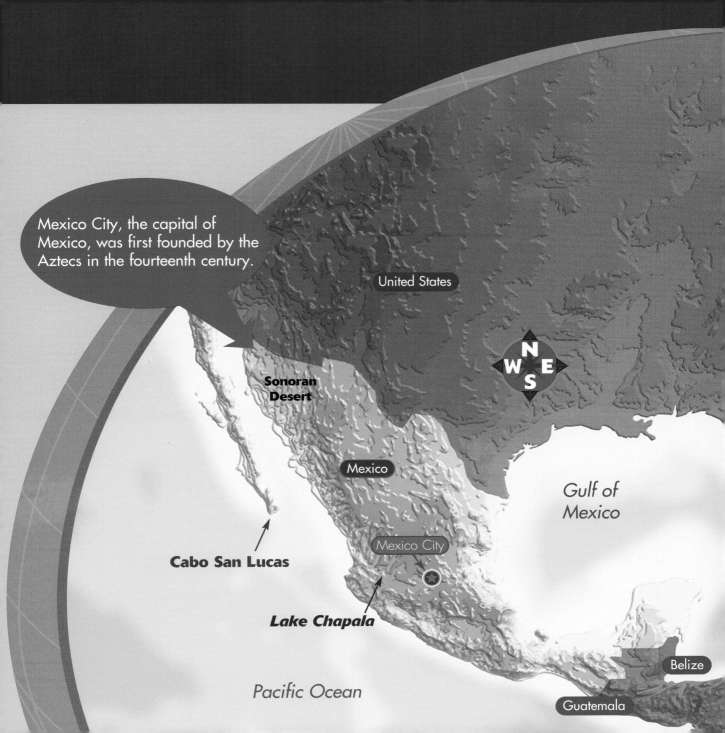

Mexico City, the capital of Mexico, was first founded by the Aztecs in the fourteenth century.

United States

Sonoran Desert

Mexico

Cabo San Lucas

Lake Chapala

Mexico City

Gulf of Mexico

Belize

Guatemala

Pacific Ocean

N W E S

Physical Features

There are many physical regions in Mexico. The central plateau has fertile farmland. It is located between two mountain ranges—the Sierra Madre Occidental and the Sierra Madre Oriental. The Gulf Coast plain is made up of coastal swamps and lagoons, dry areas in the north, and rain forests in the south. The Yucatán Peninsula is covered by jungle in the south. Baja California Peninsula, in northwest Mexico, is very dry and mountainous. The Southern Highlands contain the Sierra Madre del Sur Mountains, along the southwest Pacific coast. Chiapas Highlands contain many rain forests. The Pacific lowlands make up a dry, narrow area in western Mexico.

Mexico's climate is very warm with moderate or low rain in most areas. The rainy season is between May and October, when Mexico can be hit by hurricanes.

The Agua Azul waterfalls are located in Chiapas in the southeast of Mexico.

Cabo San Lucas is at the southern end of the Baja California Peninsula.

Lake Chapala, the largest lake in Mexico, is fed by the Lerma River.

Each winter millions of monarch butterflies make their home in central Mexico.

The Gila monster lives in the Sonoran Desert in the north of Mexico.

Sea lions are found in the waters of the Gulf of California.

The northwest is made up of deserts that get only about five inches (12 centimeters) of rain each year.

There is a variety of plant life in Mexico. The boojun tree grows in the Sonoran Desert. Oak, pine, and fir grow in the mountains. Cacti, agave, and mesquite grow in the north.

Many types of animals live in Mexico. The deserts are home to Gila monsters and armadillos. Monkeys and jaguars live in the jungles. Gray whales spend winters in the Gulf of Mexico. Bears, deer, coyotes, and mountain lions can be found in the Sierra Madre mountains.

Large rivers and lakes, such as the Lerma River and Lake Chapala, are found in the center of the country.

Human Features

There are over 104 million people living in Mexico. About one-fourth of them live in and around Mexico

The musicians who play mariachi music are called mariachis.

The Temple of Kukulkan was built by ancient Mayan people.

City, one of the largest cities in the world. Most Mexicans live and work in cities, where there are many factories. Only about one-third of Mexican families live in rural areas, where the main source of income is farming.

Most Mexican people are mestizos. Mestizos are descended from Spanish and Native American peoples. Ancient native people of Mexico include the Aztecs and the Mayans. Mexico's official language is Spanish. Spanish colonial architecture can be seen in Oaxaca. The Aztecs left behind large stone sculptures. Ancient Mayan cities can be seen in places such as Bonampak in Chiapas. Mexican music includes *ranchero* and mariachi. The national sport of Mexico is *charrería*, a show in which riders on horseback display riding skills.

Mexico is a republic. The people elect a president, a congress, and local leaders.

Mexicans have adapted to the sometimes harsh environment of their country in many ways. When earthquakes hit Mexico, many buildings collapse. Stronger buildings are being built to withstand earthquakes. Also, most of Mexico's land is too dry for farming. Irrigation is used to bring water to many areas for farming.

Mexicans use their natural resources to meet their needs. Oil is one of Mexico's most important natural resources. Oil fields are found in the Gulf of Mexico. Mexico is a world leader in producing silver, lead, copper, gold, zinc, and natural gas.

Farmers grow coffee, sugarcane, rice, bananas, and cotton. Corn and beans are grown in the central plateau area. Much of the livestock farming is done in the north. Henequen is a plant that is grown for its fiber, which is used to make furniture and ropes.

Many tourists visit Mexico to enjoy its beautiful beaches and warm climate. More Mexicans work in tourism than in any other industry.

Many oil fields are located in the state of Tabasco in southeast Mexico.

15

Air pollution affects the health of people living in areas such as Mexico City.

Montes Azules Biosphere Reserve and Laguna Miramar are located in Chiapas.

Like other large countries, Mexico suffers from water and air pollution, especially in its cities. Water pollution results from toxic materials being dumped into rivers. Motor vehicles cause much of the air pollution. Mexico City is covered by smog and has the worst air pollution problems in the country. The city is surrounded by mountains that trap the smog in the atmosphere.

Many foreign companies have opened factories in Mexico. While these factories have created jobs for many Mexicans, they have also created a great deal of pollution.

The Mexican government is concerned about the lack of clean water and the cutting down of forest trees. It has passed laws to control wastes from factories. The Montes Azules Biosphere Reserve is an area where the rain forest is protected.

4 Movement

Most of Mexico's transportation leads in and out of Mexico City. The people of Mexico use automobiles as their main source of transportation. Railroads are used to transport goods and people.

Mexico's 108 ports are used to ship goods in and out of the country. Tampico and Veracruz, the main ports, are located on the Gulf of Mexico. Ports such as Acapulco are used by cruise ships bringing tourists to Mexico. Also, airplanes are used to move people in and out of Mexico. The Benito Juárez International Airport, outside of Mexico City, is the main airport.

Mexico has over 1,200 radio stations and about 230 TV stations that provide information and entertainment. *La Journada* is a popular newspaper. Mexican artists, such as Diego Rivera, and writers, such as Carlos Fuentes, are known all over the world.

Mexico has 204,762 miles (329,532 kilometers) of highway. However, only 67,162 miles (108,087 km) of the highways are paved.

Buses are a main source of public transportation in many cities in Mexico.

Mexico is part of geographic and cultural regions. It is part of the geographic region of North America. Mexico is also within the geographic region known as the Ring of Fire that goes around the Pacific Ocean. Many earthquakes and volcanoes occur in this region.

Mexico is part of the cultural region called Latin America where people speak a Romance language. Romance languages are Spanish, French, and Portuguese. Latin America is made up of countries in the Western Hemisphere south of the United States, including the West Indies.

Mexico's land regions include the central plateau, the Gulf Coast plain, the Yucatán and Baja California Peninsulas, and the Southern and Chiapas Highlands. Mexico is divided into 31 states. Mexico's capital city, Mexico City, is considered a federal district.

The Paricutin volcano first erupted in 1943 in a cornfield in the state of Michoacán.

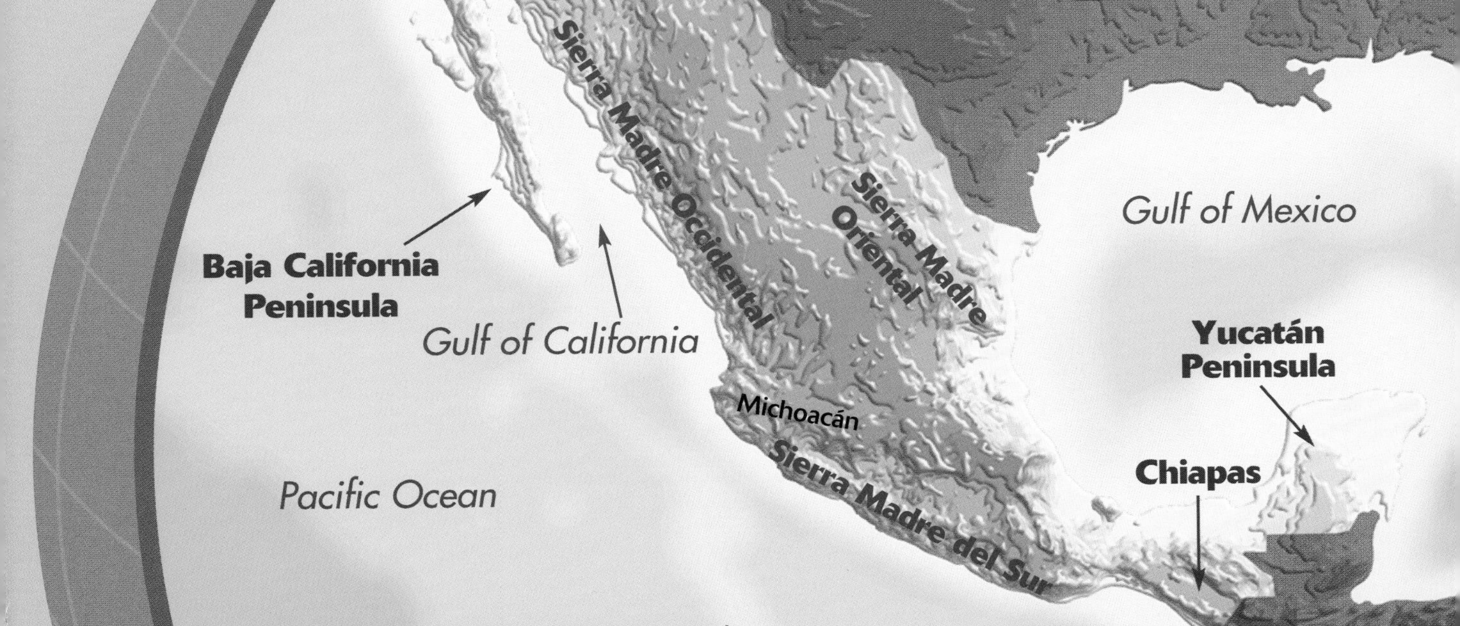

Baja California Peninsula

Sierra Madre Occidental

Gulf of California

Sierra Madre Oriental

Gulf of Mexico

Yucatán Peninsula

Michoacán

Chiapas

Pacific Ocean

Sierra Madre del Sur

The Gulf of California is also known as the Sea of Cortés.

Mexico's Flag

Population (2003) 104,907,991

Language Spanish

Absolute location 23° north, 102° west

Capital city Mexico City

Area 761,605 square miles (1,972,548 square kilometers)

Highest point Volcan Pico de Orizaba 18,410 feet (5,611 meters)

Lowest point Laguna Salada -33 feet (-10 meters)

Land boundaries United States, Guatemala, and Belize

Natural resources petroleum, silver, copper, gold, lead, zinc, natural gas, and timber

Agricultural products corn, wheat, soybeans, rice, beans, cotton, coffee, fruit, tomatoes, beef, poultry, dairy products, and wood products

Major exports manufactured goods, oil and oil products, silver, fruits, vegetables, coffee, and cotton

Major imports machinery, steel mill products, electrical equipment, automobile parts, aircraft, and aircraft parts

Glossary

descended (di-SEND-ud) To belong to a later generation of the same family.

interaction (in-tur-AK-shuhn) The action between people, groups, or things.

irrigation (ihr-uh-GAY-shuhn) When water is applied to crops by using channels and pipes.

lagoon (luh-GOON) A shallow pool of seawater separated from the sea by a narrow strip of land.

peninsula (puh-NIN-suh-luh) A piece of land that is mostly surrounded by water and is connected to a larger land area.

plateau (pla-TOH) An area of high, flat land.

region (REE-juhn) An area or a district.

republic (re-PUHB-lik) A form of government in which the people have the power to elect representatives who manage the government.

resource (ri-SORSS) Something that is valuable or useful to a place or person.

transport (transs-PORT) To move people or goods from one place to another.

23

Index

A
animals, 11
Aztecs, 13

B
Baja California Peninsula, 8, 20

E
earthquakes, 14, 20
environment, 5, 14

G
Gulf Coast plain, 8, 20
Gulf of Mexico, 6, 11, 18

H
hurricanes, 8

I
irrigation, 14

L
Lake Chapala, 11
Latin America, 20
Lerma River, 11

M
Mayans, 13
mestizos, 13
Montes Azules Biosphere Reserve, 17

N
North America, 20

O
oil, 14

P
Pacific lowlands, 8
Pacific Ocean, 6, 20
plant life, 5, 11
pollution, 17

R
rain forests, 8
regions, 4, 5, 8, 20
Ring of Fire, 20

S
Sierra Madre Occidental, 8
Sierra Madre Oriental, 8
Sonoran Desert, 11

T
transportation, 18

V
volcanoes, 20

Y
Yucatán Peninsula, 8, 20

Web Sites

Due to the changing nature of Internet links, PowerKids Press has developed an on-line list of Web sites related to the subject of this book. This site is updated regularly. Please use this link to access the list:
http://www.powerkidslinks.com/lwh/mexico